HILLSBOROUGH BRANCH

D1788755

ISBN: 978-1-85103-444-4
Originally published as *Ray Charles Découverte des Musiciens* by Editions Gallimard Jeunesse
© & ℗ 2015 Editions Gallimard Jeunesse
This edition was published in the United Kingdom by Moonlight Publishing Ltd.
36 Innovation Drive, Milton Park, Abingdon, Oxon, OX14 4RT
English text © & ℗ 2016 Moonlight Publishing Ltd
Printed in China

FIRST DISCOVERY MUSIC

Illustrated by Rémi Courgeon
Written by Stéphane Ollivier
Narrated by John Chancer

AN IMPOVERISHED CHILDHOOD

Ray Charles is born on September 23, 1930 in the Deep South of the United States. He spends the first years of his life in the most run-down area of the black neighbourhood of Greenville, Florida, where he lives with his mother, Aretha, and his baby brother, George. These

NATURAL SOUNDS

Nature has its own music: birdsong, the rustling of leaves in the wind and the sound of running water in streams and rivers. Listen carefully and try to recognise the sounds you hear around you.

At this period in the United States, African Americans did not have the same rights as white people. They were not allowed to mix with white people in school, on public transport, in theatres. They lived in ghettos, special neighbourhoods allocated to them and could only drink from specially designated water fountains (see photo above).

1. Ray Charles: Hallelujah, I Love Her So
Lonnie Johnson: Got The Blues For The West End

are the years of the Great Depression, when life is difficult for everyone, but particularly for African Americans, who are not only poor but also the victims of racial segregation. Aretha is just 17 years old. She has two children to bring up and no partner to help her. Life is tough for all three.

THE TWO BROTHERS

Ray and George are lively little boys who, once their chores are done, spend a lot of time on the street. Everybody in the neighbourhood knows them. George is good with his hands and makes toys out of bits of wood. Ray is fascinated by music. He loves

DANCING BOOGIE-WOOGIE

The rhythm is so catchy, when you listen it's hard to stay still. Doesn't it make you want to get up and dance?

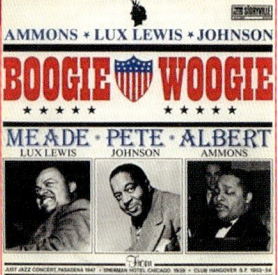

The jukebox was invented in 1930. It was a coin-operated machine which played selected records automatically, including boogie-woogie, which has a very strong, fast beat.

2 Albert Ammons: Albert's Special Boogie Woogie

to go to Mr Pitman's Redwing café and listen to the latest jazz hits on the jukebox. What he likes best is when Mr Pitman takes him on his knee and teaches him to play boogie-woogie tunes on the old upright piano. He is always welcome there.

FATE PLAYS A HAND

One day when Ray is 5 years old, he and his brother are playing together in a big laundry tub of his mother's and George drowns. Ray is devastated. Why was he not able to save him, he asks himself over and over. The question preys on his mind for years to come. Soon

MUSIC AS A COMFORT

Music can change the way we feel. It has the power to make us dream and dance but also to console us. Have you ever felt cheered up by listening to music?

Gospel song emerged at the end of the 19th century from a mixture of traditions in the African-American church. Much of 20th century music such as the blues, rhythm'n'blues and soul, is inspired by gospel music.

3 Louis Armstrong: Nobody Knows The Trouble I've Seen

something else begins to trouble him. Why are his eyes all gummed shut when he wakes up each morning? He seems to be having more and more difficulty seeing clearly each day. Could this be God punishing him?

A BLACK VEIL...

A diagnosis confirms their worst fears: Ray has an eye condition that is soon to make him blind. He is 7 years old when his mother sends him to the Florida School for the Deaf and Blind for children in St Augustine. Life is not easy for him, but Ray is clever and resourceful. He is quick to learn to read braille, but what really excites him are the music lessons. He discovers classical music, learns to play the piano, organ and saxophone, and is interested in every sort of music, from Chopin's romantic piano pieces to the frenzied swing of piano virtuoso Art Tatum.

PLAYING BY EAR ALONE

Musicians mainly use their ears when playing music. But they also use their eyes to see the piano keys, read the musical score and the lyrics of the song. Try playing a tune from memory on the piano without ever looking at your hands. Tricky, isn't it?

Art Tatum, virtuoso blues piano player, had an outstanding memory, and sight problems, just like Ray.

At the Florida School for the Deaf and Blind in St Augustine, Ray learns to read braille (opposite) and also to play a number of different instruments. He is curious about everything to do with making music.

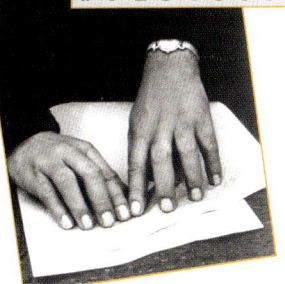

Braille is a method of reading using touch, invented in 1844. Each braille letter is made up of between 1 and 6 different raised dots. Braille enables non-sighted people to read perfectly.

ALL ALONE IN THE WORLD

Ray is growing up fast, and music is key to his existence. In his early teens on visits to his mother, at Christmas and in the summer holidays, he takes the opportunity to go and listen to jazz bands in the clubs. The idea of becoming a professional musician attracts

5 Louis Jordan: Choo Choo Ch'Boogie
Mahalia Jackson: Sometimes I Feel Like A Motherless Child

him. He secretly imagines himself on stage, playing piano. Life at school seems dull and boring by comparison. Then tragedy strikes again. Aretha dies suddenly. Ray is devastated. He is only 14 years old, and all alone in the world. What is to become of him?

A TOUCH OF BLUES

The blues came into being in the cotton fields of the United States at the beginning of the 20th century. They express the sadness and suffering of the slaves (hence the expression, to 'have the blues'). Do you ever play music when you feel blue?

VELVET VOICE

Very soon Ray decides to leave school and devote all his time to music. Florida's big cities, Jacksonville and Orlando, are home to a great number of jazz and rhythm'n'blues musicians. Ray decides to move to Florida and learn from them while he perfects his skills.

In the 30s, Louis Jordan (above on saxophone) was one of the first African-American musicians to be a success with white audiences.

Nat King Cole was one of the finest jazz singers of the 50s.

6 Nat King Cole: Route 66

Everyone is impressed by the determination of this young blind teenager. He shows talent in all the styles, but it is when he sits down at the piano and sings in his velvety voice, in the style of Nat King Cole, that people really sit up and take notice.

YOUR DREAM VOICE

We all have a favourite singer who we admire. Do you ever dream of singing like them, or practise in front of the mirror?

KING OF RHYTHM'N'BLUES

Ray begins to tire of Florida. When he is 18, he moves all the way to Seattle, at the opposite end of the country. In this huge city, everything is different: the climate, the food, relations between blacks and whites. How will his music be received? In 1951 Ray has his first real hit with the song *Baby Let Me Hold Your Hand*. From now on, there is no doubt about it: Ray is the new king of rhythm'n'blues!

First official portrait of Ray in 1951

7 Ray Charles:
Baby Let Me Hold Your Hand

Today

as in the past...

we listen to

and love

the music

of RAY

CHARLES

HIS LEGACY
FROM BLUES TO RHYTHM'N'BLUES!

Blues is the earliest form of music devised by African Americans who were deported as slaves to work in the cotton fields of the United States. The music expresses both suffering and protest. It is both lament and freedom song. Ray Charles, with his powerful, silky voice gives a remarkably raw poignancy to his rendering of the blues.

However, where he feels most at home is playing the counterpoint that introduces a dance beat to the blues and with it a wild light-heartedness. Ray excels in playing rythmn'n'blues.

In the 19th century, music, song and dance were rare sources of comfort for African-American slaves, stripped of their possessions, and displaced.

Ray Charles was much influenced by blues musicians such as B.B. King (opposite)

Ray was in touch with every new trend and is not afraid to experiment. The energy of his performances was electric.

| 8 | Ray's Blues (1961) | 9 | (Night Time is) The Right Time (1958) |

PURE MAGIC
THE RAY CHARLES STYLE

In 1954, Ray causes an uproar by mixing dance music and gospel. In *I Got a Woman*, he adopts the call and response pattern of African-American church services to create a dialogue between his own sensuous singing and the brass band's frenzied dance beat. This song is his first big hit.

Five years later, to a short riff on the electric piano, repeated throughout, *What'd I Say* has the public in raptures. Backed by his chorus group, the Raelettes, Ray takes his music to a whole new level of passion and intensity.

What'd I say is a hit from the moment it comes out. Its feverish pace has everyone on their feet, dancing.

In African-American church services, prayer times were often interspersed with gospel songs which expressed both the misery of slavery and the Christian hope of a better life to come.

PRAYER MEETING

10 I Got A Woman (1954) **11** What I'd Say (1959)

AN OUTSTANDING VOICE
CROONER

Ray Charles rapidly establishes himself as a remarkable singer of jazz ballads, giving vent to a whole range of intense emotions. *Hard Times* is a masterly mixture of tenderness, suffering, and seduction.

But it is his heart-wrenching rendering of *Georgia On My Mind* that gains him worldwide fame as a talented crooner. The devastating intensity and range of his languid, velvety soft voice touches into whole new depths of untapped emotion.

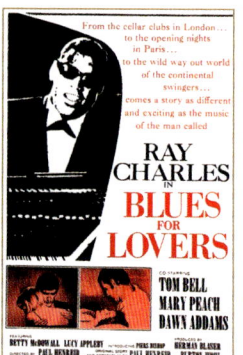

1960 marked the beginning of a golden age for Ray Charles. He performed in a string of live concerts and even appeared on film at the cinema in 1964.

Ray's re-make of *Georgia on My Mind*, written in 1930, touched the heart and soul of both black and white America, with the result that the song was later interpreted by a number of stars, amongst them Ella Fitzgerald (right)

12 Hard Times (1961) **13** Georgia On My Mind (1960)

A COLOURFUL GENIUS
BLACK AND WHITE

Popular with black and white audiences alike, from now on Ray Charles combines in his repertoire a mixture of variety songs and pieces from the African-American tradition. His re-rendering of *Bye Bye Love*, is Ray's first venture into country music, and proof of his ability to adapt to every style. However, the soul songs, like *Hit The Road Jack*, which Ray continues to compose are what earn him the title of the 'Genius' of popular African-American music. A title that goes unchallenged until his death in 2004.

The film *Ray* (2004) tells the incredible story of the man who came to be known as the 'Genius'.

A tribute to Ray Charles in the French newspaper, *Libération*, at the time of his death.

14 Bye Bye Love (1962)   **15** Hit The Road Jack (1962)

MOONLIGHT PUBLISHING

Translator:
Penelope Stanley-Baker

English narration recording:
John Chancer

GALLIMARD JEUNESSE

Gallimard Jeunesse Musique:
Paule du Bouchet

Artistic direction:
Élisabeth Cohat

Layout:
David Alazraki

LIST OF ILLUSTRATIONS

4t Water fountain for blacks only, Halifax, North Carolina in 1938, photo by John Vachon, © Rue des Archives / BCA. **4b** Map of the United States, © Géoatlas, Graphi-Ogre, 2000. **6l** American Wurlitzer juke-box, 1947-8, with 24 selections, © Bettmann /Corbis. **6c** Jazz band in a night club in Harlem. Photo by Hansel Mieth / The LIFE Picture Collection, © Getty Images. **6r** Record sleeve of 45 rpm *Boogie Woogie*, recorded in 1976, © Storyville Records. **8m** Congregation members singing Gospel, © TopFoto / Roger-Viollet. **11tl** Pianist Art Tatum (1909-1956) at the piano in the 1940s, © Lebrecht / Rue des Archives. **11bl** View of the dormitories of the Florida School for Deaf and Blind African-American children in St Augustine, 1936, © State of Florida Archives (USA), Florida Memory. **11br** Card showing Braille alphabet invented by Louis Braille in 1821 © Stefan Sollfors / SuperStock / Corbis. **11br** Ray Charles reading Braille in the studio circa 1965. Photo Michael Ochs Archives, © Getty Images. **14l** Louis Jordan (centre), jazz saxophonist, in 1948 with his band T6, © Rue des Archives / AGIP. **14r** Nat King Cole with a juke-box playing his music, end of the 1940s, © Rue des Archives / BCA. **16** Portrait of Ray Charles in 1951, © Dalle. **18t** African Americans working in a cotton field in the State of Georgia (USA),© Corbis. **18ml** Photograph of B.B. King in 1948, © Michael Ochs / Corbis. **18cr** Record sleeve of Ray Charles with photo dating from 1948, © Classics Blues & Rhythm. **18b** Dance break for farm workers of the Farm Security Administration (FSA) of Bridgeton, New Jersey. Photograph by John Collier, June 1942, © Granger NYC / Rue des Archives. **19** Ray Charles and his band playing at the Salle Pleyel, Paris, 1969, © Guy Le Querrec / Magnum Photos. **20t** Record sleeve of 45rpm record of *What'd I Say*, © Atlantic. **20m** 45rpm record of *I Got A Woman* © Atlantic. **20b** Prayer meeting of one of the African American congregations where gospel songs were sung. 19th century engraving, © Roger-Viollet. **21** Ray Charles with the Raelettes, in the mid-60s, © Michael Ochs / Corbis. **22t** A Poster for the film *Blues for Lovers* by Paul Henreid with Ray Charles, 1966 ©, Rue des Archives / BCA. **22m** Ray Charles (on piano) and his band, with the Raelettes, playing *Ballad in Blue,* also known as *Blues for Lovers* , in 1964, © Michael Ochs / Corbis. **22b** Photo of a young Ella Fitzgerald, © Corbis. **23** Ray Charles on piano performing *Blues for Lovers* (or *Ballad in Blue*) by Paul Henreid en 1966, © Rue des Archives / BCA. **24t** Poster for film, *Ray,* directed by Taylor Hackford, starring Jamie Foxx in 2004, © Rue des Archives / BCA. **24m** Poster for Ray Charles concert with the Raelettes in Hamburg, (Germany), October 17 and 19, 1970 © D. R. **24b** Front page news in the French newspaper *Libération* the day after Ray Charles's death (10 June, 2004, Beverly Hills) © *Libération.* **25** Ray Charles in the studio during a recording session, March 16, 1990. Photo from the LIFE Picture Collection, © Getty Images.

KEY: **t**= top **m**=middle **b**=bottom
 r=right **l**=left

CD

1 **Hallelujah, I Love Her So (1957)**
(Ray Charles - Gerald Wilson)
Cecil Payne: bass saxophone – David 'Panama' Francis: drums – Donald Wilkerson: saxophone solo- Joe Bridgewater and Joshua 'Jack' Willis: trumpet – Paul West: bass guitar
In 'Ray Charles or Hallelujah, I Love Her So' Atlantic

Got the Blues For The West End (1937) (traditional)
Guitar blues: Lonnie Johnson

2 **Albert's Special Boogie Woogie (1944)**
Piano: Albert Ammons

3 **Nobody Knows The Trouble I've Seen (1938)**
(traditional)
Louis Armstrong: trumpet

4 **I Got The Rhythm (1944)**
(G. Gershwin - I. Gershwin)
Art Tatum: piano

5 **Choo Choo Ch'Boogie (1946)**
(Denver Darling - Milton Gable - Vaughn Horton)
Louis Jordan and his band Tympany Five

Sometimes I Feel Like A Motherless Child (1956)
(D. Heyward)
Mahalia Jackson: vocals
The Falls-Jones Ensemble

6 **(Get Your Kicks On) Route 66 (1946)** (B. Troup)
Nat King Cole: vocals and piano
Oscar Moore: guitar
Johnny Miller: bass

7 **Baby Let Me Hold Your Hand (1950)** (Ray Charles)
Ray Charles: vocals and piano
Oscar Moore: guitar
Johnny Miller: bass
Los Angeles, 24/11/1950

8 **Ray's Blues (1961)**
(Ray Charles)
Ray Charles: vocals and piano – Frank Mitchell and Wallace Davenport: trumpet – Joe Tillman: tenor saxophone- Lloyd Lambert: bass guitar - O'Neil Gerald: alto saxophone - Oscar Moore: drums - Warren Bell: additionnal saxophone
In 'The Genius Sings the Blues' Atlantic

9 **(Night Time is) The Right Time (1958)**
(Napolean Brown - Ozzie Cadena - Lou Herman - Ray Charles)
Ray Charles: vocals and piano - Bennie 'Hank' Crawford: bass saxophone - David 'Fathead' Newman: saxophone solo - Edgar Willis: bass guitar - Lee 'Ricky' Harper and Marcus Belgrave: trumpet - Margie Hendrix: vocals - Milt Turner: drums - The Raelettes (Gwen Berry, Margie Hendrix, Priscilla 'Pat' Moseley Lyles & Ethel 'Darlene' McCrea): choir
In 'Ray Charles at Newport' Atlantic

10 **I Got A Woman (1954)**
(Ray Charles - Renald Richard)
Ray Charles: vocals and piano - Charles 'Clanky' Whitley and Joe Bridgewater: trumpet - David Newman: saxophone additionnel - Don Wilkerson: tenor saxophone- Glenn Brooks: drums - Jimmy Bell: bass guitar - Wesley Jackson: guitar
In 'Ray Charles or Hallelujah, I Love Her So' Atlantic

11 **What I'd Say (1959)**
(Ray Charles)
Ray Charles: vocals and piano - Bennie 'Hank' Crawford and David 'Fathead' Newman: tenor saxophone – Edgar Willis: bass guitar - Marcus Belgrave: trumpet - Milt Turner: drums - The Raelettes (Gwen Berry, Margie Hendrix, Priscilla 'Pat' Moseley Lyles & Ethel 'Darlene' McCrea): choir
in 'The Greatest Hits of Ray Charles' Atlantic

12 **Hard Time (1961)**
(Ray Charles)
Ray Charles: vocals and piano - David Newman: bass saxophone - Joe Bridgewater and Riley Webb: trumpet - Roosevelt Sheffield: bass guitar - William Peeples: drums - Ann Fisher, Donald Wilkerson and David 'Fathead' Newman: choir
In 'The Genius sings the Blues' Atlantic

13 **Georgia On My Mind (1960)**
(Hoagy Carmichael - Stuart Gorrell - Ralph Burns)
Ray Charles: piano - vocals
In 'The Genius Hits The Road' ABC Paramont

14 **Bye Bye Love (1962)**
(F Bryant - B Bryant)
Ray Charles: piano - vocals
ABC- Paramont
In 'Modern Sound in Country and Western Music' ABC Paramont

15 **Hit The Road Jack (1962)**
(Percy Mayfield- Charles)
Ray Charles: piano - vocals
In 'Ray Charles Greastest Hits' ABC Paramont

FIRST DISCOVERY MUSIC

JOHANN SEBASTIAN BACH
LUDWIG VAN BEETHOVEN
HECTOR BERLIOZ
FRYDERYK CHOPIN
CLAUDE DEBUSSY
GEORGE FRIDERIC HANDEL
WOLFGANG AMADEUS MOZART
HENRY PURCELL
FRANZ SCHUBERT
PYOTR ILYICH TCHAIKOVSKY
ANTONIO VIVALDI

LOUIS ARMSTRONG
RAY CHARLES
ELLA FITZGERALD